Favorite Bible Stories

Vol. 1

Retold by Christopher Brown

Illustrated by Michael Fleishman

Copyright © 1985 Antioch Publishing Company
Made in the United States of America
ISBN 0-89954-378-2

Antioch Publishing Company
Yellow Springs, Ohio 45387

THE CREATION

This is how God made the world. On the first day He said, ''Let there be light.'' Then He divided the light from the darkness, calling the darkness night and the light day.

On the second day God made the heavens.

On the third day God separated the waters and made dry land with mountains, valleys, streams, ponds, and rivers. He filled the Earth with forests and orchards, meadows and prairies. Flowers bloomed and fruit trees blossomed.

On the fourth day God created the sun, the moon, and the stars.

On the fifth day God filled the seas with living creatures, everything from giant whales to tiny crabs. Then, seeing the empty air, God made birds of every kind. They flocked and soared under the clouds, their sweet music gladdening God's heart.

On the sixth day God created all the other creatures that inhabit the Earth: lions, tigers, bears, sheep, cattle...every beast, every insect. Then, still not satisfied, God made a man and a woman. He made them in His own image and set them above all the other creatures of the Earth. God blessed them, saying, "Be fruitful and multiply."

And God was pleased with all He had done. But He was also very tired. So, on the seventh day, God rested.

DANIEL IN THE LIONS' DEN

Daniel and his people were captives of the king of Babylon. Now the king liked Daniel, who was handsome and wise. The king, Darius, heaped honors on Daniel even though he was a foreigner and a captive. The high officials of Babylon were jealous and plotted to destroy the young ruler.

"This Daniel is always talking about the God of Israel," they said. "He does not worship our gods despite the favor he has found in our land. Somehow we must find a way to use this against him."

So the high officials of Babylon put their heads together and came up with a plan to discredit Daniel.

"Oh, Great King," said the high officials to Darius, "there is much confusion and hard times in the land. Our gods do not favor us. We recommend that you set down a royal decree forbidding anyone but you to pray to any god. This will avoid confusion."

Taking their advice, Darius the king signed his name on the decree. Henceforth, everyone but the king was forbidden to pray on pain of death.

The high officials knew, of course, that Daniel, who loved the Lord, would continue his daily worship. Sure enough, spies caught Daniel praying to God and dragged him before the king.

Darius, who loved Daniel, was grieved, but the laws of Babylon had to be obeyed. Daniel was sentenced to the lions' den where he would surely be torn to pieces.

The next morning, Darius rushed to the mouth of the lions' den. He hoped against hope that Daniel was still alive.

"Daniel," Darius called, "has God saved you?"

"Yes, Your Highness," Daniel called back. "An angel of the Lord protected me."

Overjoyed, Darius embraced Daniel and placed him over all the people in Babylon. Thereafter, Daniel's God became the God of Babylon, too, and everyone prospered.

DAVID AND GOLIATH

David the shepherd boy walked into King Saul's camp. He was bringing a present of bread and cheese to his brothers, who were soldiers of the king. Across the valley the tents of the enemy could be seen. King Saul was at war with the Philistines.

David's brothers were grateful for the food. They ate together on a grassy hillside and talked gloomily about the war. Every day, they said, the Philistine champion Goliath crossed the valley to challenge King Saul.

"Will no one fight him?" asked David.

"No," his brothers answered. "All who see Goliath fear him. He is a giant nearly ten feet tall."

David looked at the glittering array of Saul's troops. Swords, spears, and helmets gleamed in the sun. That one Philistine soldier should frighten so powerful an army was shameful.

"I shall fight this Goliath myself," David declared. With that he marched off to King Saul's tent.

At first the king laughed at this upstart shepherd boy. "Go home, child," he said, "and tend your sheep."

But David was determined. "The Lord will protect me," he said. Saul finally agreed and David walked out of camp and down into the valley where Goliath waited.

"Ha! Look what comes!" the giant bellowed. "A puppy! Do you mock me, sending a mere boy to challenge me?"

Goliath was a truly frightening sight. Huge and muscular, he carried a shield the size of a tabletop and waved a spear as long as a flagstaff. David's only weapon was the sling with which he defended his flock of sheep.

Fitting a stone into his sling, David ran forward. Goliath raised his spear, but before he could strike, the whistling pebble struck him between the eyes. Down he went like a fallen tree.

Seeing their champion destroyed, the Philistine army fled. King Saul gave David a hero's welcome. The courage of the shepherd boy who trusted in the Lord was a lesson to all who heard of his wonderful victory.

THE STORY OF JONAH

One day God spoke to Jonah. "Go to the city of Nineveh," He commanded, "and tell the people there to change their evil ways, or I will punish them."

Jonah had heard frightening tales of that wicked city and did not want to go. Thinking he could escape his responsibility to God, he boarded a ship, intending to sail as far away from Nineveh as he could get.

But there is no hiding from God. No sooner had the ship left port than a violent storm arose. Huge waves tossed the little ship. The wind ripped away the sails, and the crewmen feared for their lives.

"Why has God sent this terrible storm?" they demanded.

Jonah knew only too well. "I disobeyed God," he confessed, "and now I am being punished. In order to save yourselves, you must cast me into the sea."

Reluctantly the sailors did as Jonah insisted. At once the tempest ceased. Jonah watched the ship sail away from him.

Suddenly a shadow appeared beneath the surface of the water. A great fish rose up, its mouth wide open. In another instant, Jonah was enclosed in darkness. The fish had swallowed him whole!

For three days and three nights Jonah prayed to God from the belly of the fish. God heard Jonah's prayer and took pity on him. He commanded the fish to spit up Jonah onto dry land.

As Jonah lay at the edge of the sea, God said again, "Go to Nineveh and speak against the wickedness." This time Jonah obeyed.

Jonah spoke so convincingly that the people of Nineveh gave up their evil ways. God saw the change in them and was pleased. Thanks to Jonah, the city of Nineveh was saved.

THE END